Make
BILL PAYING
SIMPLE
With This Monthly Planner!

Bill Log

_____________ Month

✓	Date Paid	Bill Name	Amount	Due Date	Confirmation

Notes

Bill Log

_______________ Month

✓	Date Paid	Bill Name	Amount	Due Date	Confirmation

Notes

Bill Log

________________ Month

✓	Date Paid	Bill Name	Amount	Due Date	Confirmation

Notes

Bill Log

_____________ Month

✓	Date Paid	Bill Name	Amount	Due Date	Confirmation

Notes

Bill Log

_______________ Month

✓	Date Paid	Bill Name	Amount	Due Date	Confirmation

Notes

Bill Log

_______________ Month

✓	Date Paid	Bill Name	Amount	Due Date	Confirmation

Notes

Bill Log

_________________ Month

✓	Date Paid	Bill Name	Amount	Due Date	Confirmation

Notes

Bill Log

_______________ Month

✓	Date Paid	Bill Name	Amount	Due Date	Confirmation

Notes

Bill Log

____________ Month

✓	Date Paid	Bill Name	Amount	Due Date	Confirmation

Notes

Bill Log

________________ Month

✓	Date Paid	Bill Name	Amount	Due Date	Confirmation

Notes

Bill Log

_________________ Month

	Date Paid	Bill Name	Amount	Due Date	Confirmation

Notes

Bill Log

_______________ Month

✓	Date Paid	Bill Name	Amount	Due Date	Confirmation

Notes

Bill Log

_______________ Month

✓	Date Paid	Bill Name	Amount	Due Date	Confirmation

Notes

Bill Log

_______________ Month

✓	Date Paid	Bill Name	Amount	Due Date	Confirmation

Notes

Bill Log

______________ Month

✓	Date Paid	Bill Name	Amount	Due Date	Confirmation

Notes

Bill Log

_______________ Month

✓	Date Paid	Bill Name	Amount	Due Date	Confirmation

Notes

Bill Log

______________ Month

✓	Date Paid	Bill Name	Amount	Due Date	Confirmation

Notes

Bill Log

_______________ Month

✓	Date Paid	Bill Name	Amount	Due Date	Confirmation

Notes

Bill Log

_______________ Month

	Date Paid	Bill Name	Amount	Due Date	Confirmation

Notes

Bill Log

_______________ Month

✓	Date Paid	Bill Name	Amount	Due Date	Confirmation

Notes

Bill Log

_______________ Month

✓	Date Paid	Bill Name	Amount	Due Date	Confirmation

Notes

Bill Log

_____________ Month

✓	Date Paid	Bill Name	Amount	Due Date	Confirmation

Notes

Bill Log

_______________ Month

✓	Date Paid	Bill Name	Amount	Due Date	Confirmation

Notes

Bill Log

Month

✓	Date Paid	Bill Name	Amount	Due Date	Confirmation

Notes

Bill Log

_______________ Month

✓	Date Paid	Bill Name	Amount	Due Date	Confirmation

Notes

Bill Log

_________________ Month

✓	Date Paid	Bill Name	Amount	Due Date	Confirmation

Notes

Bill Log

__________ Month

✓	Date Paid	Bill Name	Amount	Due Date	Confirmation

Notes

Bill Log

_____________ Month

✓	Date Paid	Bill Name	Amount	Due Date	Confirmation

Notes

Bill Log

_______________ Month

✓	Date Paid	Bill Name	Amount	Due Date	Confirmation

Notes

Bill Log

__________ Month

✓	Date Paid	Bill Name	Amount	Due Date	Confirmation

Notes

Bill Log

_______________ Month

✓	Date Paid	Bill Name	Amount	Due Date	Confirmation

Notes

Bill Log

_______________ Month

✓	Date Paid	Bill Name	Amount	Due Date	Confirmation

Notes

Bill Log

____________ Month

✓	Date Paid	Bill Name	Amount	Due Date	Confirmation

Notes

Bill Log

_____________ Month

✓	Date Paid	Bill Name	Amount	Due Date	Confirmation

Notes

Bill Log

______________ Month

✓	Date Paid	Bill Name	Amount	Due Date	Confirmation

Notes

Bill Log

_______________ Month

✓	Date Paid	Bill Name	Amount	Due Date	Confirmation

Notes

Bill Log

_______________ Month

✓	Date Paid	Bill Name	Amount	Due Date	Confirmation

Notes

Bill Log

_______________ Month

✓	Date Paid	Bill Name	Amount	Due Date	Confirmation

Notes

Bill Log

___________ Month

✓	Date Paid	Bill Name	Amount	Due Date	Confirmation

Notes

Bill Log

__________ Month

✓	Date Paid	Bill Name	Amount	Due Date	Confirmation

Notes

Bill Log

____________ Month

✓	Date Paid	Bill Name	Amount	Due Date	Confirmation

Notes

Bill Log

___________ Month

✓	Date Paid	Bill Name	Amount	Due Date	Confirmation

Notes

Bill Log

_______________ Month

✓	Date Paid	Bill Name	Amount	Due Date	Confirmation

Notes

Bill Log

__________ Month

✓	Date Paid	Bill Name	Amount	Due Date	Confirmation

Notes

Bill Log

_______________ Month

	Date Paid	Bill Name	Amount	Due Date	Confirmation

Notes

Bill Log

_______________ Month

✓	Date Paid	Bill Name	Amount	Due Date	Confirmation

Notes

Bill Log

__________________ Month

✓	Date Paid	Bill Name	Amount	Due Date	Confirmation

Notes

Bill Log

_______________ Month

✓	Date Paid	Bill Name	Amount	Due Date	Confirmation

Notes

Bill Log

_____________ Month

✓	Date Paid	Bill Name	Amount	Due Date	Confirmation

Notes

Bill Log

_______________ Month

✓	Date Paid	Bill Name	Amount	Due Date	Confirmation

Notes

Bill Log

________________ Month

✓	Date Paid	Bill Name	Amount	Due Date	Confirmation

Notes

Bill Log

_______________ Month

✓	Date Paid	Bill Name	Amount	Due Date	Confirmation

Notes

Bill Log

_________________ Month

✓	Date Paid	Bill Name	Amount	Due Date	Confirmation

Notes

Bill Log

___________ Month

✓	Date Paid	Bill Name	Amount	Due Date	Confirmation

Notes

Bill Log

________________ Month

✓	Date Paid	Bill Name	Amount	Due Date	Confirmation

Notes

Bill Log

____________ Month

✓	Date Paid	Bill Name	Amount	Due Date	Confirmation

Notes

Bill Log

_________________ Month

✓	Date Paid	Bill Name	Amount	Due Date	Confirmation

Notes

Bill Log

_______________ Month

✓	Date Paid	Bill Name	Amount	Due Date	Confirmation

Notes

Bill Log

_______________ Month

	Date Paid	Bill Name	Amount	Due Date	Confirmation

Notes

Bill Log

_______________ Month

✓	Date Paid	Bill Name	Amount	Due Date	Confirmation

Notes

Bill Log

______________ Month

✓	Date Paid	Bill Name	Amount	Due Date	Confirmation

Notes

Bill Log

_______________ Month

✓	Date Paid	Bill Name	Amount	Due Date	Confirmation

Notes

Bill Log

_______________ Month

	Date Paid	Bill Name	Amount	Due Date	Confirmation

Notes

Bill Log

________________ Month

	Date Paid	Bill Name	Amount	Due Date	Confirmation

Notes

Bill Log

____________ Month

✓	Date Paid	Bill Name	Amount	Due Date	Confirmation

Notes

Bill Log

_______________ Month

✓	Date Paid	Bill Name	Amount	Due Date	Confirmation

Notes

Bill Log

_____________ Month

	Date Paid	Bill Name	Amount	Due Date	Confirmation

Notes

Bill Log

_______________ Month

✓	Date Paid	Bill Name	Amount	Due Date	Confirmation

Notes

Bill Log

Month

✓	Date Paid	Bill Name	Amount	Due Date	Confirmation

Notes

Bill Log

________________ Month

✓	Date Paid	Bill Name	Amount	Due Date	Confirmation

Notes

Bill Log

______________ Month

✓	Date Paid	Bill Name	Amount	Due Date	Confirmation

Notes

Bill Log

_______________ Month

✓	Date Paid	Bill Name	Amount	Due Date	Confirmation

Notes

Bill Log

_________________ Month

✓	Date Paid	Bill Name	Amount	Due Date	Confirmation

Notes

Bill Log

_________________ Month

✓	Date Paid	Bill Name	Amount	Due Date	Confirmation

Notes

Bill Log

_____________ Month

	Date Paid	Bill Name	Amount	Due Date	Confirmation

Notes

Bill Log

__________ Month

✓	Date Paid	Bill Name	Amount	Due Date	Confirmation

Notes

Bill Log

__________ Month

✓	Date Paid	Bill Name	Amount	Due Date	Confirmation

Notes

Bill Log

______________ Month

✓	Date Paid	Bill Name	Amount	Due Date	Confirmation

Notes

Bill Log

_______________ Month

✓	Date Paid	Bill Name	Amount	Due Date	Confirmation

Notes

Bill Log

__________ Month

✓	Date Paid	Bill Name	Amount	Due Date	Confirmation

Notes

Bill Log

____________ Month

✓	Date Paid	Bill Name	Amount	Due Date	Confirmation

Notes

Bill Log

_______________ Month

✓	Date Paid	Bill Name	Amount	Due Date	Confirmation

Notes

Bill Log

_____________ Month

✓	Date Paid	Bill Name	Amount	Due Date	Confirmation

Notes

Bill Log

_____________ Month

✓	Date Paid	Bill Name	Amount	Due Date	Confirmation

Notes

Bill Log

_______________ Month

✓	Date Paid	Bill Name	Amount	Due Date	Confirmation

Notes

Bill Log

_______________ Month

✓	Date Paid	Bill Name	Amount	Due Date	Confirmation

Notes

Bill Log

_____________ Month

✓	Date Paid	Bill Name	Amount	Due Date	Confirmation

Notes

Bill Log

_______________ Month

✓	Date Paid	Bill Name	Amount	Due Date	Confirmation

Notes

Bill Log

_________________ Month

✓	Date Paid	Bill Name	Amount	Due Date	Confirmation

Notes

Bill Log

_______________ Month

	Date Paid	Bill Name	Amount	Due Date	Confirmation

Notes

Bill Log

_______________ Month

✓	Date Paid	Bill Name	Amount	Due Date	Confirmation

Notes

Bill Log

__________ Month

✓	Date Paid	Bill Name	Amount	Due Date	Confirmation

Notes

Bill Log

Month

✓	Date Paid	Bill Name	Amount	Due Date	Confirmation

Notes

Bill Log

_________________ Month

✓	Date Paid	Bill Name	Amount	Due Date	Confirmation

Notes

Bill Log

_______________ Month

	Date Paid	Bill Name	Amount	Due Date	Confirmation

Notes

Bill Log

_______________ Month

✓	Date Paid	Bill Name	Amount	Due Date	Confirmation

Notes

Bill Log

_________________ Month

	Date Paid	Bill Name	Amount	Due Date	Confirmation

Notes

Bill Log

______________ Month

✓	Date Paid	Bill Name	Amount	Due Date	Confirmation

Notes

Bill Log

_________________ Month

	Date Paid	Bill Name	Amount	Due Date	Confirmation

Notes

Bill Log

 _______________ Month

✓	Date Paid	Bill Name	Amount	Due Date	Confirmation

Notes

Bill Log

_________________ Month

✓	Date Paid	Bill Name	Amount	Due Date	Confirmation

Notes

Bill Log

_______________ Month

✓	Date Paid	Bill Name	Amount	Due Date	Confirmation

Notes

Bill Log

_______________ Month

✓	Date Paid	Bill Name	Amount	Due Date	Confirmation

Notes

Bill Log

________________ Month

✓	Date Paid	Bill Name	Amount	Due Date	Confirmation

Notes